RONALD RUMP

How a Spoiled, Entitled, Blustery
Little Boy Became President

J.K. HAYES

AuthorHouse™
1663 Liberty Drive
Bloomington, IN 47403
www.authorhouse.com
Phone: 1 (800) 839-8640

Published by AuthorHouse 04/11/2019

ISBN: 978-1-7283-0399-4 (sc)
ISBN: 978-1-7283-0400-7 (hc)
ISBN: 978-1-7283-0398-7 (e)

Library of Congress Control Number: 2019903111

Print information available on the last page.

authorHOUSE®

RONALD RUMP

How a Spoiled, Entitled, Blustery
Little Boy Became President

WRITTEN BY J.K. HAYES

OVERVIEW

Ronald Rump, How A Spoiled, Entitled, Blustery Little Boy Became President is a book that examines the political conditions in the United States that enabled the election of an inept, inexperienced, egomaniacal narcissist. The story is written and illustrated in the format of a children's book intended to remind readers about how we elected a person so incredibly unqualified for the office of president.

The political context for this book highlights the strategic decision of the Republican Party to intentionally withdraw its participation from any Obama initiatives and actively obstruct his ideas for short term political gain. Additionally, the book points out the Democratic Party's inability or unwillingness to embrace, advocate, or explain Obama era policies.

Congressional approval during the Obama administration was at an all-time low. Political infighting, fiscal cliffs, and government shutdowns, amplified by a media that calculates winners and losers rather than policy and outcomes, became the new norm. Because of these forces, Trump was elected.

Further, the book reminds us of the speech and tweets of Donald Trump. His vitriol went unchecked by elected leaders and normalized a tone that undermines our values and ideals. Many of the elected leaders in Washington D.C. have put grandstanding, gridlock, and their own re-elections ahead of doing the peoples' business.

Once upon a time, in the greatest country in the world, the first African American was elected president. At the time of his election, the country was in the midst of the greatest recession since The Great Depression.

Nevertheless, the country was hopeful.

But, the Republican Party was not interested in working with the new president. The Republicans held a private meeting the night Obama was inaugurated and made a pact to actively oppose any of his ideas. Republicans were determined to make Barack Obama a one-term president.

And, Republicans stuck together. When the president wanted to fix health care, he tried to work with the Republican Party. He even adopted *their* plan to improve health care. Republicans still... said... no.

Mitt Romney, the Republican presidential nominee who originally implemented "Obamacare" in Massachusetts, ran on a platform of repealing it.

Essentially, Republicans didn't want to pass legislation that might make the president look good.

This dismissive attitude toward Barack Obama was not new.

When asked about the prospect of Mr. Obama becoming president, Congressman Steve King said:

"The Al Qaeda, and the radical Islamists, and their supporters will be dancing in the streets in greater numbers than they did on September 11th."

Characterizing Obama as "other", "foreign", and "Muslim" was amplified by the Republicans' deafening silence.

Outrageous claims by elected officials about Obama didn't end there. Politicians like Sarah Palin continued to slander the president.

Sarah Palin

"The America I know and love is not one in which my parents or my baby with Down syndrome will have to stand in front of Obama's 'death panel' so his bureaucrats can decide, based on a subjective judgment of their 'level of productivity in society,' whether they are worthy of health care. Such a system is downright evil."

One Republican politician, Joe Wilson, even called the president a liar during a joint session of Congress.

A storied American actor, on national television, during the Republican National Convention participated in the new norm of disrespecting the President of the United States.

And Republicans remained quiet.

In spite of all of the Republican obstruction, there was a lot that the Obama administration accomplished.

- The Recovery Act supported infrastructure projects and kept teachers, fire fighters, and first responders employed.
- The auto industry bailout was producing better cars and increased employment.
- The Affordable Care Act insured more than 20 million people. And people could not be denied health care because of a pre-existing condition.
- The war in Iraq ended.
- President Obama made the decision to launch the operation to kill Osama Bin Laden.
- The administration doubled the production of renewable energy.
- Wall Street was reformed through the Consumer Protection Act.
- President Obama repealed Don't Ask Don't Tell.
- The Lily Ledbetter Fair Pay Act was signed.
- The Unemployment rate went from 10% during the Great Recession to 4.7% by the time President Obama left office.

But Democrats didn't help much. In spite of all this progress, they didn't confidently embrace or explain their own policy positions, or the president's agenda.

Their spinelessness left many people wondering what Democrats stand for.

As the Republicans gained power in the House of Representatives, they spent their time voting to repeal the Affordable Care Act.

By January 2016, congress voted over 60 times, to *repeal and replace* Obamacare, knowing that President Obama would never sign the legislation. All those votes cost tax-payers millions of dollars.

Republicans were addicted to dysfunction and had an enormous appetite for obstruction. In 2013, they even shut down the government for **17 days**.

A lot of time and money continued to be wasted.

Sadly, when 4 Americans lost their lives at the U.S. Embassy in Benghazi, Egypt, Republicans, with their congressional majority, spent more than two years and 7 million dollars investigating Secretary of State, Hillary Clinton.

Eight committees, including the House Select Committee, concluded no wrong doing on the part of Secretary Clinton or the Obama administration.

Republican House Majority Leader Kevin McCarthy touted the investigation as a success.

He claimed the investigation a success, not because of what was learned or how we might be able to prevent future harm to American diplomats, but because, in his words:

"Everybody thought Hillary Clinton was unbeatable, right? But we put together a Benghazi special committee, a select committee. What are her *numbers* today? Her *numbers* are dropping."

Speaking of numbers...

Obstruction in Congress was unprecedented. Congress was the least productive and the least popular in history.

Congressional Job Approval -- Full Trend

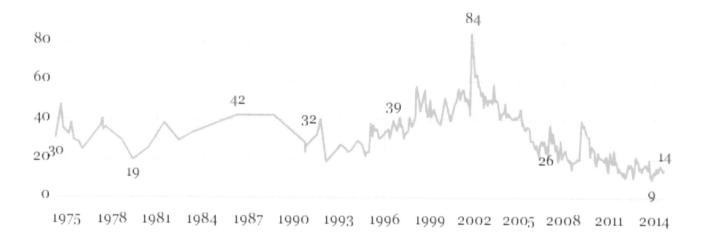

GALLUP

All the HOPE and CHANGE of the Obama Era turned into frustration and cynicism.

By 2016, some people were willing to be lead by *anyone*.

Along came Rump. And he was talented. He was *great* at finding the things that could divide people and *great* at convincing some voters that he knew anything at all.

So, he began to question the citizenship of the first African American president.

Rump was finally getting the attention he had always been told he deserved. And, he was going to prove that he could be a big boy. So he decided to run for president. He was going to put his talents of ignorance, inflated ego, divisiveness, and dishonesty to good use.

When Rump announced his candidacy for president, he made it absolutely clear how he felt about Mexican people.

"When Mexico sends its people, they're not sending their best. They're not sending you. They're not sending you. They're sending people that have lots of problems, and they're bringing those problems with [them]. They're bringing drugs, they're bringing crime, they're rapists, and some of them, I assume, are good people."

" I will build a great, great wall on our southern border and I will have Mexico pay for that wall. Mark my words."

Rump's childlike disposition compelled him to respond to questions in an infantile way.

Reporter: "John McCain, five and a half years as a POW and you call him a dummy. Is that appropriate in running for president? He's a war hero."

Rump: "He's a war hero? He's not a war hero. He's a war hero because he was captured. I like people who weren't captured, okay."

On the campaign trail, Rump was eager to share his bigotry and lies.

"I want surveillance of these people. I want surveillance, and, I don't' care. I want, are you ready for this folks, are you ready? Oh they're going to make it such a big deal. There going to make it so big! He said something so politically incorrect. That's why we're going to hell because we are so politically incorrect. Such a big deeeeaaal. I want surveillance of certain Mosques okay. If that's okay. I want surveillance. We've had it before and we'll have it again.

I watched when the World Trade Center came tumbling down. And I watched in Jersey City, New Jersey, where thousands and thousands of people cheering, so something is going on, we've got to find out what it is..."

Rump also argued that a federal judge could not do his job because of his ethnic background.

Reporter: "If you are saying that he can not do his job because of race, is that not the definition of racism?"

Rump: "No, he's proud of his heritage, I respect that…"

Reporter: "You're saying he can't do his job because of it."

Rump: "He's proud of his heritage. Look, I'm building a wall. I think I'm going to do very well with Hispanics. You know why I'm going to do well with Hispanics, because I'm going to bring back their jobs. They're going to get jobs right now. But we're building a wall. He's a Mexican. We're building a wall between here and Mexico. The answer is he is giving us very unfair rulings. Rulings that people can't even believe… The best lawyers, I have spoken to so many lawyers, they said this is not a case, this is a case that should have ended. This judge is giving us unfair rulings. Now I say why. Well, I'm building a wall. And it's a wall between Mexico, not another country."

Reporter: "He's not from Mexico. He's from Indiana."

Rump: "He is of Mexican heritage, and he's very proud of it."

When concerns about a presidential candidate not releasing his taxes were raised, Rump assured the country in a tweet:

"Tax experts throughout the media agree that no sane person would give their tax returns during an audit. After the audit, no problem!"

Why would a person running for president not want people to see his taxes?

Rump's misogynist disposition was on full display during the Republican debates.

Megan Kelley: You've called women you don't like fat pigs, dogs, slobs, and disgusting animals. Does that sound to you like the temperament of a man we should elect as president?

The next day...

Rump: The fact is, she asked me a very inappropriate question. She should really be apologizing to me if you want to know the truth. You could see there was blood coming out of her eyes, blood coming out of her wherever.

Rump explained his grotesque predilections on Howard Stern's radio show when he said,

"I'll go backstage before a show, and everyone's getting dressed and ready. And I'm allowed to go in because I'm the owner of the pageant, and therefore I'm inspecting it...

Is everyone okay? You know they're standing there with no clothes. "Is everybody okay?"

"And you see these incredible looking women, and so I sort of get away with things like that."

And who could forget his most infamous statement when he explained his tendency to sexually assault women?

"I better use some Tic Tacs in case I start kissing her. You know I'm automatically attracted to beautiful- I just start kissing them. It's like a magnet. Just kiss. I don't even wait. And when you're a star they let you do it. You can do anything.

Grab them by the pussy. You can do anything."

One might think that all of these egregious, disgusting behaviors would have disqualified Rump from being president, but many were frustrated with the "Do Nothing Congress."

And, according to Rump, he is really rich. Some equate wealth to intelligence and ability. So Rump *must* be right when he says,

"Nobody knows the system better than me, which is why I alone can fix it."

And with most of our cable news coverage and political talk radio resembling a reality T.V. show *atmosphere* where political infighting is the norm - Why not elect a reality T.V. show *host* for president?

And so we did...Even though he didn't win the popular vote. (Hillary Clinton had almost 3 million more votes).

Most people were shocked. Many were devastated.

A candidate that made put-downs, outrageous claims, racism, birtherism, sexism, and stupidity central to his candidacy, convinced just enough people that he could get something done in Washington D.C.

What does it say about our country that a candidate with no political experience, and no grasp of history or policy, could be elected?

Would this have been possible in a political climate where politicians focused on the peoples' business rather than on their own re-elections?

Rump's inauguration had a very different tone than President Obama's inauguration. In his inaugural address Rump declared "This American carnage stops right here right now."

But Rump had inherited much better circumstances than his predecessor and insisted that the country was in shambles. Even though the economic conditions had greatly improved during the Obama administration. The unemployment rate dropped from 10 percent to 4.7 percent. There were also 75 straight months of job growth during the Obama administration– the longest streak on record.

Job Growth Under the Obama Administration

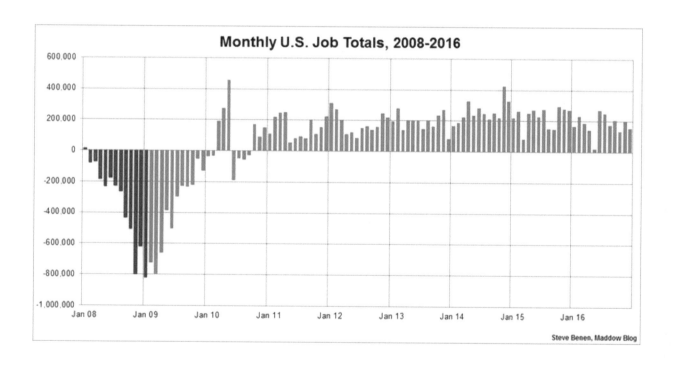

The night of Rump's inauguration, he had his press secretary, "Spicey" tell us that he had the largest crowd size in history – Period!

One might wonder what else Rump is lying about…

REFERENCES

Obama, Barack. "Obama's Inaugural Address: The Full Text." *Time*, Time Inc., 20 Jan. 2009, content.time.com/time/politics/article/0,8599,1872715,00.html.

Eisen, Norman, et al. "Why Steve King Keeps Winning." *POLITICO Magazine*, 16 Mar. 2017, www.politico.com/magazine/story/2017/03/why-steve-king-keeps-winning-214913.

Kessler, Glenn. "Sarah Palin, 'Death Panels' and 'Obamacare'." *The Washington Post*, WP Company, 27 June 2012, www.washingtonpost.com/blogs/fact-checker/post/sarah-palin-death-panels-and-obamacare/2012/06/27/gJQAysUP7V_blog.html?utm_term=.2cc6728b8527.

Abdullah, Halimah. "Eastwood, the Empty Chair and the Speech Everyone's Talking about - CNNPolitics." *CNN*, Cable News Network, 31 Aug. 2012, www.cnn.com/2012/08/31/politics/eastwood-speech/index.html.

thegrio.com/2012/03/16/the-road-weve-traveled-watch-obama-2012-campaign-film/.

Walsh, Deirdre. "House Votes to Repeal Obamacare; Sends Bill to Obama - CNNPolitics." *CNN*, Cable News Network, 7 Jan. 2016, www.cnn.com/2016/01/06/politics/house-obamacare-repeal-planned-parenthood/index.html.

McAuliff, Michael. "House Republicans Spent Millions Of Dollars On Benghazi Committee To Exonerate Clinton." *The Huffington Post*, TheHuffingtonPost.com, 29 June 2016, www.huffingtonpost.com/entry/benghazi-report-clinton_us_57727ed2e4b017b379f74880.

tpmtv. "Kevin McCarthy: Benghazi Committee Tanked Hillary's Poll Numbers." *YouTube*, YouTube, 30 Sept. 2015, www.youtube.com/watch?v=x8Wff2-IKkA.

Gallup, Inc. "Congress Job Approval Starts 2014 at 13%." *Gallup.com*, 14 Jan. 2014, news.gallup.com/poll/166838/congress-job-approval-starts-2014.aspx.

Date, Ian SchwartzOn. "Trump: Mexico Not Sending Us Their Best; Criminals, Drug Dealers And Rapists Are Crossing Border." *Video | RealClearPolitics*, 16 June 2015, www.realclearpolitics.com/video/2015/06/16/trump_mexico_not_sending_us_their_best_criminals_drug_dealers_and_rapists_are_crossing_border.html.

CBS News. "Donald Trump Won't Call John McCain a War Hero." *CBS News*, CBS Interactive, www.cbsnews.com/video/donald-trump-wont-call-john-mccain-a-war-hero/.

"Donald Trump's Full CNN Interview with Jake Tapper - CNN Video." *CNN*, Cable News Network, 3 June 2016, www.cnn.com/videos/politics/2016/06/03/donald-trump-hillary-clinton-judge-jake-tapper-full-interview-lead.cnn.

He has claimed that ongoing IRS audits prevent him from doing so. "All the Things Donald Trump and His Team Have Said about Releasing His Tax Returns." *CNNMoney*, Cable News Network, money.cnn.com/2017/04/17/news/donald-trump-tax-returns/index.html.

FoxNewsInsider. "Donald Trump and Megyn Kelly Go Back and Forth at the Fox News GOP Debate." *YouTube*, YouTube, 6 Aug. 2015, www.youtube.com/watch?v=1Y9_LJj7A68.

Ian. "Trump on Megyn Kelly: 'There Was Blood Coming Out Of Her Eyes, Blood Coming Out Of Her Whatever' During Debate." *Video | RealClearPolitics*, www.realclearpolitics.com/video/2015/08/07/trump_on_megyn_kelly_there_was_blood_coming_out_of_her_eyes_blood_coming_out_of_her_whatever_during_debate.html.

Kaczynski, Andrew. "Donald Trump to Howard Stern: It's Okay to Call My Daughter a 'Piece of Ass'." *CNN*, Cable News Network, 9 Oct. 2016, www.cnn.com/2016/10/08/politics/trump-on-howard-stern/index.html.

kolapkansorn. "Grab Them by the Pussy Donald Trump." *YouTube*, YouTube, 21 Jan. 2017, www.youtube.com/watch?v=PwWux5BAczk.

rdcleaners. "Trump Says No More Crime and I Alone Can Fix It." *YouTube*, YouTube, 30 July 2016, www.youtube.com/watch?v=LUwnus4DulA.

Benen, Steve. "Obama Era Ends with Steady Job Growth." *MSNBC*, NBCUniversal News Group, 6 Jan. 2017, www.msnbc.com/rachel-maddow-show/obama-era-ends-steady-job-growth.

Printed in the United States
By Bookmasters